Praise for SCYTHE

"Why would any of us refuse what we desire now?" asks Marie Antoinette of the speaker of *Scythe*. In this sharp book of poems by Elizabeth Sylvia, we walk unsteady through the twin fallen kingdoms of the interior and the exterior, with Marie Antoinette as our Virgil. There is compelling conflict in this book between the desire to live fully and experience the whole world, and the desire to preserve said world by extricating ourselves from it. So we look seriously, gravely, at motherhood and dwindling butterflies, at pyrocumulus clouds from wildfires, at the expensive dogs we buy in order to love them. We wonder how actually one praises a world in line for the guillotine, and arrive at no easy answers. But I do love the answer Sylvia's speaker gives: "I am still devoted to the grass beneath our feet."

—ANDREW HEMMERT, author of *No Longer at This Address*

"In our contemporary neo-liberal world order, it can be difficult, if not impossible, to imagine beyond a relentless and reckless complicity. But seeing through the tacky gilding is a first step. Enter Elizabeth Sylvia's *Scythe*, a remarkable poetry collection about Marie Antoinette and her legacy that considers with refreshing honesty and insight what it costs to live at the heart of an empire and feast on its spoils."

—KATHRYN NUERNBERGER, author of *HELD: Essays in Belonging*

"The best historical poetry is also timely; it moves beyond the subject into the symbolic. Elizabeth Sylvia does this and more. In *Scythe*, Marie Antoinette steps out of time. As readers, we experience the last Queen of France's voice through expertly crafted persona and surprising contemporary turns and musings. We walk with her through a modern garden. Marie even watches *Real Housewives.* Sylvia's brilliant juxtaposition of the past and present reflects the darker realities of modern comfort, of clinging to the belief that, 'history happens far' away. It is about our own opulence and excess, how we are 'wild-eyed to keep it.' *Scythe* is historical poetry, but it is also a personal and ecopoetical cry to not let the 'finite goods of this jeweled planet [run]/ through our fingers.' In this hall of mirrors, Sylvia asks us to confront how like Marie Antoinette we all are. How much worse."

—SARA MOORE WAGNER, author of *Lady Wing Shot*

SCYTHE

ELIZABETH SYLVIA

RIVER RIVER BOOKS  *Durham, North Carolina*

cythe

Published in the United States of America

Library of Congress Cataloging-in-Publication Data
Sylvia, Elizabeth, 1974–
Scythe / Elizabeth Sylvia.
ISBN-13: 979-8-9926116-1-8
Subjects: LCSH: American Poetry, New England, Environment, Women's Literature, Marie Antoinette.
LCGFT: Poetry.
LCCN: 2025939950

Cover and interior design by Alban Fischer
Cover art adapted from Élisabeth Louise Vigée Le Brun's *Marie Antoinette in Court Dress*, 1778. Public domain.

RIVER RIVER BOOKS
10 Linganore Place
Durham, NC 27707

www.riverriverbooks.org

CONTENTS

NOTE TO READERS

The poems in this collection make frequent reference to the Hameau de la Reine, or Queen's Hamlet, a private retreat on the grounds of the Versailles Palace which Marie Antoinette used for her personal entertainment. The Hameau included several faux rustic buildings and a small model farm near the gardens of the Petit Trianon, an informal palace designated for Marie's use.

We had a beautiful dream and that was all.

—MARIE ANTOINETTE

An American family of four has more hired help than the Sun King at Versailles.

—NATHANIEL RICH

HARVEST

Pulling ripe berries
from the u-pick bush,
Amy says,
If there is such
a thing as Heaven,
which I doubt,
it is an orchard
filled with fruit.

I love this too,
her daughter adds,
although it
makes me feel
like Marie Antoinette
on her fake farm.

I'm reminded
of my honeymoon,
wandering Versailles
and the Queen's
costume gardens,
germ of my first child
deep in the pocket
of my womb.

INVITATION TO MARIE ANTOINETTE

Walk once again around the yard with me,
before the autumn's early frost pulls down
my garden's ornaments. Though we've both known
the little darks of sleep, I'm not ready
for forever or thereafter. I've heard
you grew religious once this bloody world
had shaken heel of you but I am still
devoted to the grass beneath our feet,
to heirloom chickens, honeybees, the wall
of pines that shields me from society.
Will I linger in some future person's
past the way that you persist in mine?
See that mantis on the seed-head's golden
throne? She too readies for the end of times.

SÉCHERESSE

3000 miles apart, Marie's hamlet
and mine raise the same dust ghosts
beneath each human step. Grass so brittle
it begs for fire from an errant spark.

The fountains at Versailles run low
and Paris shimmers in the heat,
a corset of days above a hundred degrees.
I'd like to walk in my bare feet

on a carpet of deep jade but I won't
water my lawn and the newspaper's map
flames my whole state with the orange
of drought. Still, I bring the hose

to my beds of flowers, reluctant
to forgo their rainbow bursting,
the promise in their soft plump buds.
Green is every living thing's

color of refuge: sunshine and shadow,
water and air. I breathe beneath the same
lace-leafed oaks that shelter the catbird
and the silent hare. As at Versailles,

the leaves already yellow here,
are dry enough to crackle underfoot.
My daughters rush to stomp on them
and crush their papery cups to rings of soot.

BRIAR

Drought sears the tip
of the blackberry
—the stunted fruits
crunchy as old turds.

But closer to the stem
the bloodblack drupes
grow sweeter than
they've ever been.

Premature
nostalgia makes
every berry metaphor
for loving a dying place.

The way Ted told me
his parents, divorcing,
fucked like rabbits
in the guest room.

This occupied us.
We were young and had
the golden bodies of gods,
gorged honey and sunlight.

I could not imagine,
then, taking hold
of what I had chosen
to release.

Despite summer's
deep juice blossoming
the briar, calling
forth the bee,

heat and the years
have pricked me.
I see the future's
dry well rising.

POUF

Because she loves the thistle and the black-eyed Susan's
golden ruff, Marie Antoinette flutters the meadow

to tease me with her new coiffure. Those outlandish
poufs were her own hair, not wigs, at least until her hair

began to crack like desiccated grass. I'm tallying
the drought and shaking dust off of the weeds

I won't allow to prosper in the desert ground.
The Queen's amused by my anxieties. In place of feathers

or the naval ships she bore in life, she's made her hair
a patch of flame that swirls around a redwood tree.

I say *I don't think that's funny.* Her eyes
regard me from below the titian tower,

and she answers *I'm not the one who set this globe*
on fire. It's all of you, gambling three planets' lifetimes

every day. Why would any of us refuse
what we desire now? We are the last

queens of the coming revolution and should dance.
I keep on pulling mugwort from the sandy dirt

hoping only the native plants will grow—
they can't compete against this rhizomous invader.

Marie approves. *See*, she says, *even now you are choosing*
what deserves to flourish, what can be beautiful.

WOULD YOU RATHER

Would you rather never be able to hug me again
or go everywhere with me riding on your back?
My daughter makes a game of such questions.

Would you rather live in a house accessible only by ladders
or in a house one foot underwater? Last night,
we watched the new *Dune.* In it, a groundskeeper
pours water at the roots of a palm tree. The thirst of each
palm would water fifty men for a day. *Should we*
remove them? asks Paul, slim scion of the new imperial house
come to press its gilded rule upon the spice-rich sands.
No, says the groundskeeper. *These are sacred.*

Would you rather die by being shot into the sun or swallowed
by a giant space worm? Scientists record unearthly temperatures,
nights holding the heat like a bag over the world's head.
Picturing *Dune's* sand worm, the absoluteness of those dark bowels,
I sense the slow belly, the last constricting geologic months,
know I'd choose a reckless slingshot to the sun.

FLIGHT

We take flight too many times a year, but most reliably at winter's squalid tail, when schools free children for one dismal week and we break New England's seal to find some paradise.

Each year we pass that week away from winter in France's colonized *départment* of Guadeloupe, from which the native people all were cast though some of their volcanic names remain.

We light at Petit Havre, handful of sand beneath the coconut palms where my girls snorkel round the seagrass paths and leap the little cliff to surf the left-hand break of gentle waves.

French sandwiches of bread and buttered ham beneath the palm trees. Waters blue as curaçao.

Every year fewer butterflies succeed the thousand-mile crossing to their winter's peace. I watch the monarchs wake on YouTube, trees seeming to blossom when they rise.

THE SCYTHE

I bought it made to order, wooden-joined,
three-foot hammered blade
tailored to my measurements:
shoulder, hip, length of leg, and so
when I take it up the meadow—
that mix of weed and wildflower
scrabbling in the sand above the leaching field—
and start to swing, it moves
like a part of my own body arcing before me.
My yoga teacher would envy
how I loose my arms and pivot,
tilting my hip and sending the blade
skimming over soil like a shearwater
edging the waves. The scythe is quiet work,
and faster than the gas-fed trimmer I can't
pull long enough to start. I fell spent
flower stalks and spires of seeding mugwort
in an hour of warm work, time enough
to catch the startled flight of a yellow warbler
winnowing a coneflower, dragonfly
and grasshopper flashings. Years ago
a summering New York mother at swim lessons
told me she envied my slower pace of life
and this must be what she meant:
the simplicity of one task, done
not even well but for itself,

my body like a loaf of bread rising
with its joyful parody
of peasant song, $400 scythe
leveling the path before me.

CATALPA

The blossom Amy plucks off the ground,
she says, reminds her of Ohio.

She never sees the heart-leaf tree around
these neighborhoods out East where she's lived for

nearly thirty years, but I look down
the road dusted with dropped flowers

imagining the three-foot pods to come.
I know her strange tree well. My neighbor's

yard harbors a giant specimen
that in a winter storm might cleave our

house in half and summers blocks the sun
with such passion that nothing grows under

it. Wherever the seeds land, they begin
sprouting fingering roots with the vigor

of hateful ideas. The foundation
of a house won't survive them, I tell her,

they return no matter how much you pull them.
That's the way such wolfish things always are.

LA CONCIERGERIE

In the yard, a monarch full past season
lands upon a zinnia. I planted the flower
that misled him. It should be wilted
on the compost heap, he winging
towards Mexico. With age a butterfly's wings
tatter, the filaments unclasping, fabric ripped
from overuse. Two months in the darkness, Marie
wore the same dress, forgot what the color white
was meant to be, missed an escape plot
hidden in a flower. She tells me to keep looking,
says, *You don't know shit until you've lain in it.*
Marie knew her own death was coming, the only logic
of such early night. *My Protestant forebears thought*
this whole green earth a dunghill, I remind her. At every
ending: mud and piss on the floor, a man calling the names
of the extinct, the endangered species list growing
shorter as whole families are removed.

FLIGHT

In Guadeloupe's warm sun I open like a flower. We wear our swimsuits at the table, watch the skittering green lizards cross the patio, snorkel at the Jacques Cousteau reserve, angelfish sequins scattered in the water.

Flight and flee descend from the same English origin.

Home is the opposite and goal of flight. In Guadeloupe, I watch the spotted eagle ray conduct his shadow 'cross the sea's illuminated floor although my being there will drive him further out.

When I talk about escape, I mean vacation, plane wing over the tropics, carbon emissions sailing me somewhere warm enough to distract me, not yet warm enough to make life difficult.

JARDIN, 1793

Sunny days Marie puts on
her *bergère's* cap and comes
to walk the yard with me. She loves

to think of how the trees might have
entwined some secret *amoureux*
the year she died. I tell her that those
trunks are gone, the hemlock
and red spruce. Who knows

if they stood even then, or if
the colonizing stamp of field
and dry-stone fence already marked
this place. White men logged

its native name, which means
A Place of Rest, upon America's
new maps but splintered
the Wampanoag with King Philip's War.
Whatever I now call my own took root
upon those violences. Marie rebuffs

reminders of such harm, summons
polished wampum strands, the flashing
music of a jingle dress. Birdsong
and the supple leaf-greened light conspire

to her silences. Despite their history,
Marie will look upon these woods
and think, *A wilderness.*

MAY THE ODDS BE EVER IN YOUR FAVOR

My daughter wants to dress as Katniss Everdeen for Halloween
and we make her costume, black leggings and spray paint:
Katniss in the second *Hunger Games*, reluctant symbol
of a rebellion she has never cared about.
I've done the same thing with my child—held her to the day
as a purpose and a promise of improvement, but then
most days I don't make the world better for children,
because I'm too busy bettering it for my own.
My friend Ruth sits on the tail of her minivan
describing the wealth she's building for her sons, impenetrable.
I know she's afraid, we all are. She is building a cistern
on the roof of her house, she's a scientist, she's telling me
the rains of the future won't fall as they do now. We'll
live perched between flood and flame. Even this week,
the water went bad somewhere in the lines and we gave up
drinking from the taps though the end of the world
hasn't even begun, at least in how we sense it. Late autumn
jeweling every green and ruby leaf, my daughter's hair
a shining honey I braid to mimic Katniss. I'm the one
who brought her here, to fix this world I keep destroying
in her future's name, knowing what I hope most is not
that everything will stop descending into chaos,
but that my own sweet ones will be among the saved,
among the safe, watching from a distance.

AT THE HOUSE, WHERE WE ALL ARE

I spend Sunday afternoon sorting
the children's clothing
from the parents'—ours—

we've worn the same banalities
over and over

they grow thin from unnoticed use, bear the stains
of forgotten crafts
my hands
feel over them halfway between beggar and queen
the way I take softness and discard it

I know I get to be safe here and do not know what I owe the unsafe

I have done little
to deserve my place, my placid chores

and what is it to listen at the television's broad mouth

history happens far from me, beyond even where interstates
cleave the territories of wild things,
menacing them in their hunger and thirst

in my own garden little rain has fallen but water rushes in the pipes

a friend's daughter scowls in the mirror, waiting fierce
            for the water wars her mother says will come,
      the years when what we take for plenty dries away

she doesn't know yet the dignity of those who will arrive
            holding their living tightly as she holds her own

slicing the boundaries we think we've made,
      dams and highways trembling and crosshatched

EGGS

Marie was an egg to be broken,
but not because the yolk was bad or good.
It was a day for making omelets. History
fell on her like a boot. She wasn't innocent,
of course, we know nobody is. The system made Marie
and it was rotten, a shell needing cracking,
dropped her yellow yolk in the judgement bowl. A chicken
is a system for making more chickens.
The goals of death or revolution are in the end
impersonal. I don't question them. Still,
hoping my own departure won't have such drama,
I'm extending my stay in this single world with organic vegetables,
weight-bearing exercise, and personal relationships.
All of which could bring me to the fire times ahead,
a future I imagine only like any movie I've already seen:
have-littles and have-nots dressed for the morning
after a Sex Pistols concert, desperate as hell
for food but still plenty of stuff to go around:
disposable straws, plastic bottles, pants
with the knees already ripped. Anyone with a garden,
with a gun, wild-eyed to keep it. Will I die sitting on the porch
with a revolver, scaring folks out of my chicken coop? If I
read the news too much, it seems a likely way to go
and if Marie had pictured M. Guillotin's precipitous device,
perhaps she never would have left for France.

But maybe she'd go on the same, resplendent
in her jewels and gowns, committed to the final dance.

FLIGHT

Marie was known to care for orphaned children, and for one small boy captured from Senegal to be her "gift." Though she unkeyed his bondage, Marie would never send him home, not even when she knew that she was set to die.

Guadeloupe's a land the French saw only for its sugarcane and rum. Children's children of those brought against their will have peopled it. Last year for the first time, despite the condo's pristine pool, no water streamed the pipes for days. My hair grew knotty from the ocean salt. This place was *Island of Beautiful Waters* for its many springs. Now islanders fill jugs because the taps run dry.

The Internet can't help me find the link between vacation and escape. When I search those words, a deck of beachside photos answers back.

What happened to Jean Amilcar, as he was known in France, his first name stolen from his mother's mouth? His was a body dropped by history. Every state shift is a tale of loss.

ON LEARNING THAT KIM KARDASHIAN EXCEEDED HER WATER ALLOWANCE BY 232,000 GALLONS IN JUNE

The guide pauses to tell her group
that when Marie Antoinette
walked these paths,
Versailles swallowed
as much water
in one day
as Paris

used in a month.
A likeness of the sun god
rises in the gardens'
central pool,
barely harnessing
his frenzied horses
of the dawn.

L.A. glistens
with elsewhere's water—
snow off the Sierras
misting the carpets of lawn,
collecting on the leaves
of imported citrus, every fruit
a globe bursting with juice.

At Versailles, too,
oranges were grown.

FUITE À VARENNES

Marie remembers the escape attempt

Even disguised
as a governess
I couldn't surrender
travelling like a queen

The green *bérliner* carriage
slow as a barge
through the unknown night
and my husband
still the *Roi*
in his valet's
garb

Like a turtle
on those golden wheels,
I carried the treasures
of my life

silver plates
that ciphered
my letters into Louis'

a carved dressing kit
with my own likeness
rampant on the pearl

two pots for the sacred
night soils
of the crown

I meant
to be known
as Queen of France
the moment my slipper
touched that ground again

Until then, the *bérliner*
lumbered on

a world contained
within a narrow window

What I knew of the world
beyond the carriage

wolves and wolves
in peasant dress

their teeth
red with desire
for my neck

and *Louis Roi* baring
his face to the crowd's sun
so that their pikes
surrounded us

For the children
it was all
a theatre

the small *Dauphin*
asleep at our feet
in his little dress

MUSÉE DES ARTS DÉCORATIF, PARIS

Room after silent
golden room,
furniture sat in by queens
and every silken surface
matching. Swans, cranes,
unicorns, table legs
carved like lions
straining under marble
tops. Untouched
and glossed to perfect
by that lack of use.
Within this filtered feed
of luxury—far as history
and fingertip close—
my daughters
speed through the tableaus
intoxicated by splendor,
picture themselves
princesses in these
glittering sets.
That is mine!
A gilded escritoire.
That is mine!
A crystalline
decanter. *That*
is for my palace!

Frantic to acquire,
each is overcome
with a child's rage
when she is not the first
to claim a silken coverlet,
an inlaid dressing box,
as adults trail behind,
at ease within these cool
and muted marble corridors.

VIDA NOVA, LOS ANGELES

A house like this has rooms you'd never enter,
rooms for wrapping gifts, those ritual

weapons of exchange the global rich bestow
because they love to see themselves reflected

in each other's eyes. At sixty thousand feet
it's just a third smaller than the Sun King's

palace at Versailles, but newer owners
need a tutelage in the great lesson of excess:

Who can live in such ungovernable space? When even
many residents are dropped into a *maison* bigger than a mall,

they sometimes flounder in their rushing affluence.
Versailles had hundreds of servants,

sometimes thousands of guests. Anyone with a rented coat
could watch the King eat supper from his golden plates.

Now the owner-class monogram their entry gates,
iron letters only readable when locked, and still

the clouds will wander carelessly away,
bearing their little plunder of the dew.

CLOISTER

Days before the end of the world,
I walk beside Marie, neither
peasant nor monarch,
all pollen, jelly, hustle, and bank.

She's there to ghost along
my boxwood bordered paths, enjoy
a queenship cloistered in the yard.

At night, Marie will come
to hive beside me in the bed.
She'll never watch the news
& says it keeps her up at night.

Television carries on its catalogue
of guns and heat, though accident of birth
has made those stories distant as the rain.

Like everyone, I'm hoping
to escape before the oceans touch
my door. The only rocket out
from here is ownership. I inch
from one dark hexagon to the next,
laying the pearls of my future in the wax
of someone else's work.

Marie keeps whispering.
We are two queens of a scorched season,
finite goods of this jeweled planet running
through our fingers, a pair of porcelain twins
glassed in our cabinet, counting down.

CAKE EATER

When Marie called for the bread-starved
to eat cake, slavery was *interdit* in France 500 years.

Except it wasn't. Angel cake, devil cake.
French colonies stole men and sucked their lives like sugar cane.

Brought to those fields, most wouldn't last
a decade. Sweetness grew on blood

and sugar's horror should
have dulled the tongue. It didn't.

Appetite shifts like a dragon on its pile of bones,
ravening tastebuds the ledger of demand.

Supply, a way to excuse the burning fields of cane,
ravaged forests, brutal heritage

so far from the refined confection I whip
to frosting white as women's powder.

Sweetness wracks the body,
smoked air fills the burning fields.

Patches of dead water bloom
downstream from the harrowed acres.

There is much damage in cake,
ambrosial and tender in my mouth.

PSL

Marie adores candied apples, jack-o-lanterns,
torches of Indian corn, fleshy pumpkins

cut with smiling faces. From the front seat
of my car, head full of pumpkin dreams,

she asks for Starbucks,
so I stop, picturing pumpkin seeds

spilling from her sectioned neck.
Her drink dispels such darkness

with a golden pump. Marie's delighted
everyone loves pumpkin spice.

She's sympathetic to a basic bitch, soft
to the marketplace's buyable delights. When fall

skitters with bad ghosts, sugar's a sweet antidote
for how the turning world keeps shortening her days.

THE STRAIGHTENING

Marie remembers being prepared for marriage

Open my mouth
for *M. le Dentiste*

the steel *pélican*
clacking in his hands

I show what it means
to be a princess
by how I submit
to pain

Blood chokes
my throat as he yanks
each pearly tooth
from its bed

I will never wonder
at the violence
of beauty or its price

Excised teeth
rattle like dice
in my palm

✣

In my mouth
a golden cage
to order what remains

Enamel soldiers
powdered ladies in wait
crushed marble *allée*

They call this straightening
Fauchard's Bandeau

I should have called it
Versailles

DELIVERY

You might picture Marie at the Opera,
the pannier wings of her court dress heavy
with elaborate stitched display,
but I've always been drawn to the private luxury
of her own hidden palace, the way a visitor must
pass the Olympian Versailles gates,
sun's omnipotence blazing every line,
cross the shadeless gardens, paths
dry and absolute despite the fountains'
arcing power, before the jewel box can be found.
                    Landscape of stark divisions and behind it,
the follies and composed tableaus, gold-flashed theater
and best of all the dainty farm with its miniature windmill.
Little scene for secrets, for quiet, for being someone
other than this life insists.
                              If a queen can have everything
and feel undone by it, let me harbor slighter shame
that sometimes I cannot resist the pleasure of delivery's brown bags.
How gently the world for one evening sets me down
when I make that simple call.

STRAWBERRIES

In the backyard sun,
Marie and I devour strawberries,

ephemeral rubies I grow
bedded on golden straw.

Four dollars would buy the same,
boxed in transparent perfection

at the grocery store. Marie
does not discriminate—

if summer berries are a pleasure,
winter berries are a pint-sized luxury.

She *neverminds* the way I fret
about their dirty lineage, knowing

I will bank my shopping cart
with their fleshy hearts,

the only fruit my American child,
my little *Dauphine* of the warming world,

will take from me, quartered to reveal
the icy white beneath their scarlet cheeks.

CHICKEN

The chicken's all organic,
pasture-raised.
Marie is *amusée*
to see me pick the dark meat
from the bone. Why
spurn the grocery's
boneless breasts, smooth
as polished rose quartz
in their perfect tray? What
explanation do I have?
This nature
is a kind of luxury.

OPEN CART

Marie remembers her execution

Death smells
only to the living

I ride
through my life
for the last time

thrown from the cell
of darkness
into the cold roar
of day

Noise
Noise

✣

They bring me
to the square

open cart
signifying
my shame

The crowds
will have their fill
of me

who once
appeared to them
a balconied ideal
in cloth of gold

No more child-
breath sweetening
my skin

No more cut
roses in a bowl

I still welcome
the sun's silent eye

ROSÉ ALL DAY OFF INTO THE SUN

after a tweet by @girl_recovery

Marie's in the drive when I get home from work,
jingling her change purse of *livres* and gold *Louis.*
I can't count her money and neither can she but while I was
ticking down the dollars at my job, she was watching
RH: Orange County, Atlanta, LA. Listen, Marie knows
we have it good here—she sees the laundry's spinning magic
and we cut flowers in the million-year-old golden light,
but television reveals refrigerators with glass doors that open
on an everlasting hoard of bottled water, chilled tumblers
for the poolside patio. Carpe drink 'em! She wants rosé
pink as a velvet hairbow, sweet as her little daughter's breath.
Wine at the kitchen island is a telescope lens of the immediate moment.
All the anger is room-sized, all the targets in reach.
Marie likes a pretty label, picks her bottles for a close-up shot
so she can guzzle *Velvet Ribbon, Daughter Breath, Do Not Remind Me*
Every Day Is a Blister in this Necklace of a Lifetime.

HEAT INDEX

Summer mornings, the house fills up with CSPAN,
hot-take comments on masking, emails, and the Supreme Court.
Marie will stay in bed if she's not up. Why quibble with the dead?
The world she knew is just as lost as ours. *You'd make a decent queen,*
she purrs to me, searching out the Property Bros with the remote
in her white royal hands. Who cares which one is Drew
and which is Jonathan—they share the pecs and mannequin teeth
of modern princes, would never try to make her sweat without a/c
the way I do, clocking the thermostat to 84°, collapsing
Marie's coif against her cheek before I'll click the magic
of cold summer wind. Marie despises talk of climate change.
We all live in a dying time, she says. So I say, *Look, HGTV,*
and power up the air. If I don't, I know I'll hear
her whole sad tale again, queen in the Tower
praying her little boy survives.

UNWRAPPING, 2006

My uterus a mirrored hall reflecting itself,
ruby velvet cushioning the smooth moonstone
of my daughter's head,

my not-yet daughter's not-born head,
stitched with the jet bead of her
coming eye

That year as the flag of my body
unfurled, a bugling fanfare
accompanied me everywhere,

and in the yard of the old city house,
our cherry tree launched
the loose confetti of its petals

So many people brought gifts that I grew
tired of unwrapping, lustrous paper
and ribbons in ruin at my feet,

each hot night presaging, as I lay before the a/c's
artificial chill, these blistering
and anxious times ahead

TEACHING MARIE ANTOINETTE TO DRIVE

—Her dainty foot takes quickly to the gas—

—It's the whip she's wanted—

—We lurch out from the drive as though the car
might rear on its hind legs—

—Who will stop us in this grand machine of shining chrome—

—Is it so much, she asks, to be powerful and free—

—Bigger than ourselves & we can own the road with what
we drive—

—I too love coming and going— —Will pause to curse
the idle drivers who detain me— —*Gros cons, the lot,*
Marie is quick to add—

—She turns her jealous eye towards bigger cars until she sees a Hummer on the road—

—Oh untouchable Glory—

—Portable fortress—Bulletproof windows—Leather seats—Wheeled throne—

—Yes, yes, that's what she wants, to be so far removed—

—What else will keep our children safe—

THE SITTING, *MARIE ANTOINETTE AND HER CHILDREN*

Marie remembers being painted by Élisabeth Vigée Le Brun

How I would love
to walk into
the moment
of this painting

and once again
be seated against
the light

to watch Élisabeth
lift up her carmined brush
and wait

the warm breath
of my children
almost visible
among the shadows
of the room

Behind me
the Hall of Mirrors
horrible

infinity of selves
and yet the light

Here in the portrait room
one beam of sun falls
into the empty cradle

My son's hand
moving to shroud
that untouched bed

I do not look
at the absence
death has laid there

I see only Élisabeth's
tender wrist flooding
the crimson of my gown
across her canvas

My daughter's length
spilling into mine
reds of our dresses
double beats in the heart

ZHUZH

Marie loves Pinterest, loves
Mommy Bloggers, loves a *zhuzh,*
stays up late watching videos,
hands full of glue guns and spray paint,
demands crafts from the dollar store
and tells me all her favorite
jewels were made of paste,
the flowers too.
You make
a beautiful tableau
and live in it.
In prison, Marie
still bought ribbons.
After her beheading young aristocrats
tied scarlet bows around their pretty necks.

BUYING IT

At least once a week I text
my best girlfriend
that I can't stop shopping,
stacking my screen
with tabs
of the things
I most want
to take possession of

Sometimes she texts back
Shop for the life you want

She knows mine's
making pottery and drinking
green juice out in Monterey
and I know hers: Palm Beach
princess with a mahogany tan

Last spring we had a lot
of talk about white jeans
and when I wore mine,
wide leg, cropped,
exposed button fly,
I did feel cool

Like I might figure out,
finally, how to drink
a cocktail on the deck
before dinner while
I was inside cooking it

And because I'm always
buying a little salvation
with my habit, those jeans
are *Made in USA,*
the mandatory
minimum wage
rinsing out
my gluttony
so I can hold those
white jeans
over my head, a flag
and a blindfold

THE FLOOR

Some days Marie
gets really down about
the *wear and tear*
that we inflict
upon this house:
chipped edge
of the porcelain sink,
grey daub of fingerprints
idling
around the knobs.
Why can't we have
hand-thrown plates,
vaulted ceilings & beams,
a woman who cleans
more than once
a week?

At Versailles
people pissed
on the floor.

THE LAST GARDEN AT VERSAILLES

Marie remembers her hamlet

This garden a world
of my own making

Every bloom
a breath freed
from its formal corset

In the distance
white billy goat
leading his seven wives
across a field
dotted with clover

When my children
tumbled
on the lawns
I ran only as their mother

I called them in
with berries and cream
from the Swiss-born cows

let roses fall wild
across my vision

their thorns
lofted against
the court's barbed tongue

Before society awoke
I might voyage to the sunrise
among my own fir trees

Alpine garden
all the mountains
I would ever know

Even the plans
a barricade

I drew
the narrowest paths
believing only love
could walk them

SCALE

Marie makes me a scale, *0 to Marie.*
Getting up at 5 am to pay
for health insurance? I tell her
that's a zero. She says, *Do you think*
I ever had a day off in my life?
Sometimes I want to argue
about privilege and she
shows me how her head
pops right off her neck.

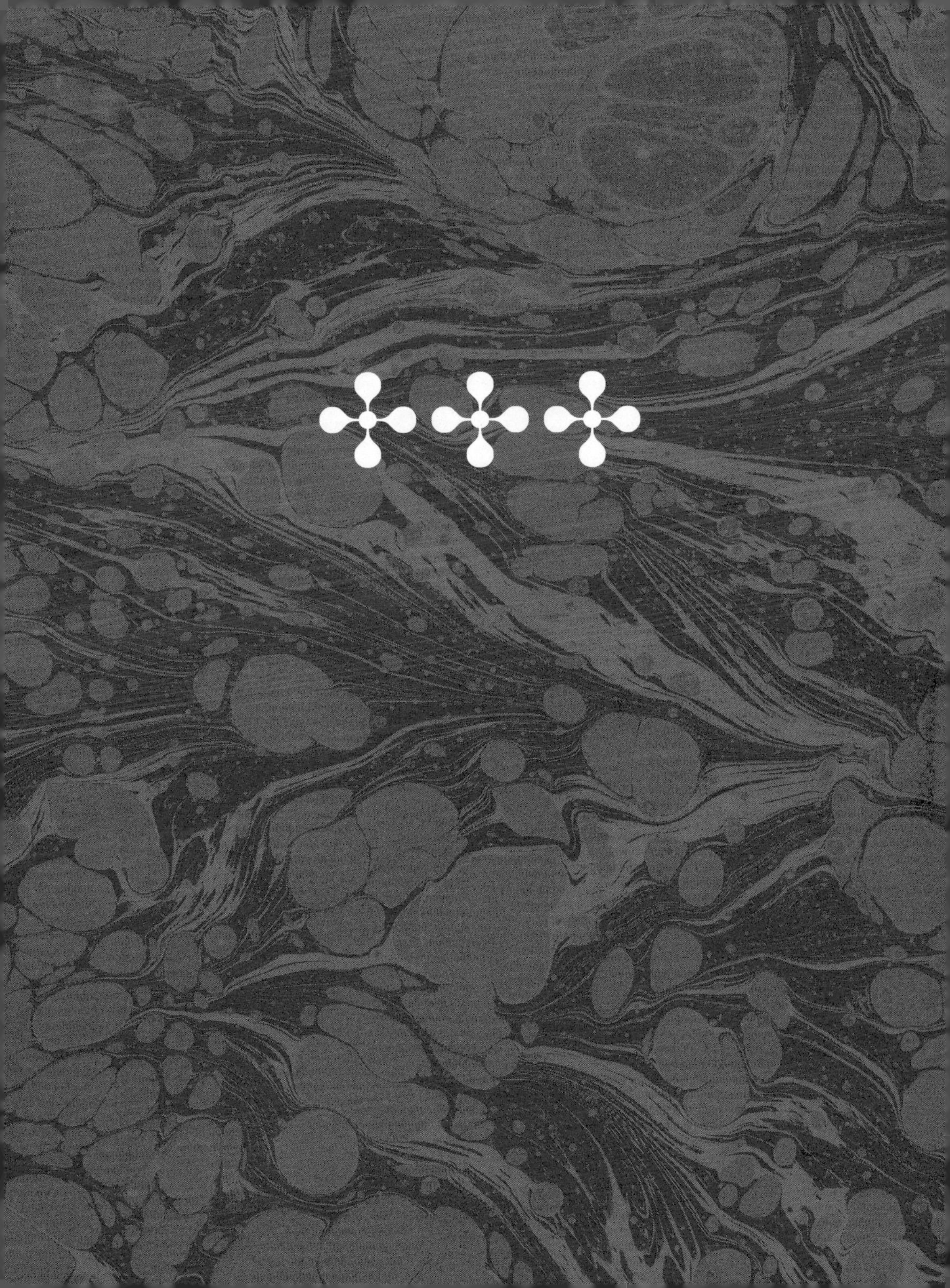

HAMEAU DE LA REINE

Marie had a farm built behind her own palace,
the *Petit Trianon*, with a pond, a windmill, sheep
white as the clouds of heaven. She did not
pretend to be a shepherdess there, despite
what gossip said. Still, her little hamlet,
like my own, was a burlesque.

What I am, I own. What I own, I am.
My *proprieté*. Marie's word did not
separate the self from its possessions,
my own soft skin, the quiet of my garden,
lawn greener than emeralds.

I think what I want is something simple,
but I want the image of simplicity
through a filtered lens:
one thing to gather an egg, another
to slaughter the pullet.

This golden afternoon glorifies a few red tomatoes,
a fanfare of zinnias, the hand-carved beehive,
color-splashed heirloom chickens
I feed from my hand.

FEEDING THE BEES

In the afternoon, I head to the meadow
to feed the bees. It's early October—
wild asters and goldenrod,
the regal fall crocus,
splayed petals like an open hand.
I've come to offer the bees thick
sugar and water. In the midst of fall's
bounty they can still starve. Though
they hum in perfect industry and society
with one another, they need a keeper's
help to hold on through the long night of winter.

I am setting this golden moment against the darkness,
for soon it will fall to another winter, and sooner
to the relentlessness of days
from which, like a bee captured by rain,
I cannot seem to emerge. I feed the hive
slowly, that the dance is not upset,
but the pleasure I take in the bees' work
I cannot always take in my own. I long
not for the transit of pollen, despite its glory,
but for the straightened confines of the hive.

ALLEGORY OF THE CAVE

There's a jay trapped
in the truck cap
my husband
has set down
on the driveway.

With furious
disbelief he flies
at the cap's
window, again,
again, refusing
to believe its
material presence.

Bang, bang, bang
against the plexi
with his
panicked wings.

He could escape
by hopping out
the way he came.
He'd need to be
more calm
to think of that,

able to see
the world
within the cap,
not just
the garnet fringe
of the maple
outside.

SAFE AS HOUSES

Even sad houses beckon me,
paint curling off the shingles, worn
at the steps. I can imagine myself
inside. I lived in an old house once,
pulled down sheets of flowered paper,
painted, polished. The only kingdom
I've ever wanted, interior.

I like to live in a house
like a yolk inside a shell: me,
the body, the room, the house,
the property line.

Inside my body, my self—
a homunculus spinning the dials
of my binocular eyes. Even the car
can be a house. Certain days

I sit in the driveway
with the doors locked,
no one knowing where I am,
the best sort of invisible.

RAIN

rain keeps falling here on the east
coast of America / the western
fires seem lunatic imaginings / rain
tells us quiet down / I feel
damp behind the knees
between the breasts

we do our part
of staying inside &
the flowers do theirs / outside
under the darkened dome / out
west the sky is also dark / a friend calls
to tell me / false clouds

formed from ash / particulates
in ongoing transubstantiation / memory
retaining the true thing that once
was / chalk drawings washing
from the driveway

I can't always give
away what is given / I want to offer
balance / am no person able to / who can
in the face of such pyres / continue

FIELD PANSY

My nectar wooed the laden bees tumbling
in the grass,

flagrant below the sun, every pistil
shuddering

as their busy legs brushed me with
fertile news

Now there is less in the air,
less show,

less reaching towards the other
So be it

Bunkered, self-contained, fed
rations

of the known, resilience burrows
each looped

gene, makes my descendants
pale duplicates

Hoarding and blameless, I drop
little pollen

in the world's begging cup,
against present

and expected loss, unfold scant
shrunken blooms

SUNDAY

It's always
Sunday in these poems.

The small, expensive dog
lying outstretched on the sunlit deck.

I hear nothing but the hum of the domestic,
laundry in the dryer, an occasional

car that passes. My neighbors
spinning through weekend chores.

For a moment the light captures everything
with a painted stillness, even sound.

Between me and the world,
a green wall of cedars,

an admonishment against looking,
looking in, and looking out.

GOOD NEIGHBORS

The young man teaching me to espalier
in the YouTube video from some Utah non-profit
is probably Mormon, considering
his mirrored sunglasses and the flat line
of his sandy blond bangs as he demonstrates how to set and wire
the posts that guide the baby tree.

Espalier's a technique for training fruit trees
so the branches stretch out flat, good for small spaces
like the walled gardens of France.
I want to grow a green blockade between myself and my neighbor,
who cleared the work that wilderness had done
across his property. Three men with machetes cut for a whole day.

For years before he moved here, I seeded an island
in a verdant sea. Now there is always the road, chainsaws, barbecues.

Under many circumstances, I might hate
this fellow in the video. He probably believes things I could never agree with
about women and gay people, but he's also sweetly showing me
how to wind an apple sapling's tender branch along a wire.

His non-profit builds gardens
in strangers' yards, which is more good than I have done for the planet
or another person today. In three or four summers, I hope

that when I look across my lawn, I'll see only the green shoulders of apple trees unloosing the small fists of their blossoms.

FALL

When the hatchling fell from the porch rafter,
I did not tell my daughter that her father
had toppled the nest. Between pricks of feathers
we saw skin less than a baby's skin, pink as the first
fragile covering on a burn. I knew its mother
would not come for it huddling on the threshold.

In the night, too small to stand, it dragged
across the porch boards with paperclip wings
until it tipped into a crack. The chick will die—
might have done so anyway, born so late
in summer that the earliest fall leaves
are drifting to the lawn.

These are things adults know. My daughter
proffers the chick in her tender hand. Instead
of mercy, of cracking its skull's light shell,
I offer suffering, stuff an old yogurt cup with tissues,
tuck the nestling back in the eaves,
lying to my child that its mother will return.

RECYCLING

I want to wash out the bottles and cans with the same hope my friend
Susan's mother had washing out the bottles and the cans

Thirty-five years ago on Long Island soaking the paper faces off her sauce
jars before the blue truck rumbled by Monday Wednesday

Friday the recycling plant closing for the weekend at five its optimistic
piles banging their song of rescued orphans

I was still a copper penny of a kid back then and Susan's mother's sink
warm and soapy with the week's glass

Though I never knew her she washed it out for me a knob of the past
snatched up for the future

She and a thousand other tidy mothers learning to worry about the mess
they would leave behind

Tying up their aprons on that recycling business so Susan can sit on the
back deck with me today

Immaculate sky seeping through every breath in summer's canopy

Threaded by birdsong and Susan's mother's long dead no way to tell her I
keep hauling the yogurt cups

To the curb despite some townspeople's complaints about the eyesore of the man-sized bins

Who will remember the care I took to scrub the peanut butter jars how I shook clean the milk

Who will remember I did all this

IL FAUT CULTIVER NOTRE JARDIN

We must cultivate our own gardens   the proper   the property
Cultivate windbreak on the inside   every familiar face with our own

Cultivate the loose-slipped nodding heads of poppy   Cultivate salvia,
        column of purple thrones for the iridescent bees

It is morning, afternoon, evening below the sun's distracted eye

& still sky holds us like a cradle, each in our egg cup,
        no part untethered, no seam ripped

Cultivate expectation between the yielding peach
        and mouth of pleasure

Cultivate the gold of almost evening on the deck as leisure bends
towards dinner, how each of us takes a task to ourselves,

                line of kebobs on the grill, char over eggplant's melting center,
                        weight of folded napkins

Cultivate this as a place apart, untimed

Cultivate blueberries, strawberries, tiny seed of a raspberry nested in its aril,
                juice like the blood of a summer morning

OH, FOR SWEETNESS IN THIS WORLD

Into the hummingbirds' saucer, I pour a mix
one part sugar, four parts water. Sweetness
and thirst: two poles that guide
the living. When the bees
exhaust summer's nectar,
I brew a sweeter one,
twice sugar in each cup
of water, so thick it slows
before spilling. At the feeder,
late-born bees tongue the syrup
that will transform to honey in the hive-
close winter days. First year of the pandemic,
my daughters and I baked fifteen pies and left them
at the doorways of our friends. Pecans captured in an amber matrix,
jaggery, honey and maple, each bite in the mouth an unbearable flooding.

NEW YEAR'S EVE WITH MARIE ANTOINETTE

The sparkling Christmas lights still hang
around the window's bitter portrait
of the early darkness and the rain.

Marie and I are tucked into the sectional's
deep corner, celebratory flutes of champagne
in our hands and firelight reflecting
in her eyes. She'll never be as old as I am now
or see one of her children
reach the age of mine. Due to the rain,
this old year's fireworks have been called off,
and so we won't be out in town
among the glittered noisy throngs,
but nestled in that private family life
Marie knew only as a Temple prisoner. For her,
It was the one time we led a life like yours,
our children near to us,
and respite from the court panopticon.

And though she knew by then that she would die,
she still imagined that her son might live
to rule in France, her loved first daughter
make some safe marriage in a far regime.

I think that this year you ought to resolve
to keep your head, she teases me.
I truly can't endorse the alternate.

Outside the Temple walls, thundering
chants for blood and revolution—
within, she read with dear Marie Therese,
or took Louis to walk the prison's garden paths.

Tonight we share some bites of lemon cake
and watch my daughters gamble penny candies
at the dining table. The new year rolls out
like a bolt of silver silk. Just this evening,
I know this is a world worth saving,
and I can listen to the rain unworried
by December's lack of snow,
our home this glowing candle in the night.

NOTES

The portrait of Marie Antoinette in this book owes to many sources but is most often drawn from ideas formed while reading Antonia Frasier's *Marie Antoinette: The Journey* (Doubleday, 2001) and Carolyn Weber's *Queen of Fashion: What Marie Antoinette Wore to the Revolution* (Picador, 2007). The images in Christian Duvernois' *Marie Antoinette and the Last Garden at Versailles* (Rizzoli, 2008) were another indispensable source of inspiration.

Epigraphs: from a letter by Marie Antoinette to the Chevalier Jarjayes; from Nathaniel Rich's review of *How the World Really Works* by Vlaclav Havel, "Everything You Thought You Knew and Why You're Wrong," in the *New York Times,* May 11th, 2022.

May the Odds be Ever in Your Favor: President Snow's benediction at the opening of the Hunger Games in Suzanne Collins' dystopian young adult trilogy of the same name, whose juxtaposition of glamourous excess and environmentally degraded destitution seems ever more prescient.

On Learning that Kim Kardashian Exceeded her Water Allowance by 232,000 Gallons in June: As reported by NPR on August 24th, 2022.

V*ida Nova*, Los Angeles: Inspired by *The New York Times* article "What to Do With a Multimillion-Dollar Megamansion? They Have Some Ideas," published November 21st, 2021.

PSL: popular acronym for the widely reviled pumpkin spice latte.

Rosé All Day off into the Sun: "Mommy wine culture is a scam. It's not cute. It's another effective attempt to subdue or annihilate women. Rosé all day off into the sun" — *@girl_recovery*

The Last Garden at Versailles: The title refers to the gardens Marie Antoinette developed by her private palace, the Petit Trianon, which included the English garden, the Alpine garden and the Queen's Hamlet. This poem borrows its title from Christian Duvernois' photobook of the same name.

Field Pansy: Inspired by the *New York Times* article "Flowers Are Evolving to Have Less Sex," published January 9th, 2024.

Il Faut Cultiver Notre Jardin: The famous axiom of Pangloss in Voltaire's *Candide.* It suggests that, rather than concern ourselves with distant events, we "must cultivate our own gardens."

ACKNOWLEDGMENTS

My appreciation to the following journals where versions of these poems first appeared:

Arc Magazine: "Chicken" "The Floor"; "Scale"; "Zhuzh" published as "o to Marie Antoinette"

A-Minor Magazine: "Pouf"

Broadkill Review: "Open Cart"; "Rosé All Day off into the Sun"

Cagibi: "Invitation to Marie Antoinette"

Carve Magazine: "Sunday"

Cherry Tree: "Hameau de la Reine"

The Dodge: "Field Pansy"; "Fall"

Feral: "Feeding the Bees"

Greensboro Review: "Sécheresse" as "Summer Drought"

Kitchen Table Quarterly: "The Straightening"

Lily Poetry Review: "Allegory of the Cave"

Noctua Review: "Catalpa"

Ohm Journal: "At the House, Where We All Are"; "The Cake Eaters"; "La Conciergerie"; "Strawberries"; "May the Odds"; "Would You Rather"

On the Seawall: "*Vida Nova,* Los Angeles"; "Heat Index"; "Teaching Marie Antoinette to Drive"

North American Review: "New Year's Eve with Marie Antoinette"

Painted Bride Quarterly: "Briar"

Passengers Press: "On Learning that Kim Kardashian Exceeded her Water Allowance by 232,000 Gallons in June"

riverSedge: "Oh, For Sweetness in This World" published as "The World is a Sucker for Sweetness"
The Southern Review: "Good Neighbors"
West Trade Ecobloomspaces Anthology: "Cloister" as "Ars Antoinettica"

REMERCIEMENTS

A thousand thanks to Han Vanderhart and Amorak Huey, who invited the return of this manuscript and understood its vision.

Thanks also to the Mattapoisett poets, who gave feedback on these poems, and my friends at the Longleaf Writer's Conference where I was a fellow in 2024—Seth Tucker and Matt Bondurant for inviting me, and Vandana Khanna and my workshop friends for their thoughtful feedback. To Jennifer Martelli for edits and encouragement. Extra thanks as always to Susan Pizzolato, my forever reader and champion, and Vivian Eyre.

Thank you to my parents, who helped me find my first French words when we lived in Algeria and abetted my complicated love for France with our many voyages there. And to Colin, Aubrey, and Catherine: loving you has given structure to my life.

And finally, thanks to Amy Pickworth and Ruby Goldstein, whose blueberry picking banter ignited the idea for this book.

ELIZABETH SYLVIA was raised on Martha's Vineyard and still lives in coastal Massachusetts. She is the author of *None But Witches* (2022), winner of the 3 Mile Harbor Press Book Award, and the chapbook *My Little Book of Domestic Anxieties* (Ballerini Books, 2025), a finalist for the Kari Ann Flickinger Memorial Prize. The daughter of an avowed Francophile, she lived in France as a young woman and continues to visit regularly.

RIVER RIVER BOOKS was founded by Amorak Huey and Han VanderHart in March 2022. Inspired by the idea that you cannot step in the same river twice, two poetry editors join together to publish (at least) two exceptional poetry titles a year, as well as the Plainwater Nonfiction Series.

Poetry Catalog

An Eye in Each Square, Lauren Camp, 2023
Bullet Points: A Lyric, Jennifer A Sutherland, 2023
Dear Memphis, Rachel Edelman, 2024
A Geography That Does Not Hurt Us, Carla Sofia Ferreira, 2024
Pastoral, 1994, Joe Wilkins 2025
Your Mother's Bear Gun, Corrie Williamson, 2025
Field Notes, E.G. Cunningham, 2025
Encounters for the Living and the Dead, Jameela F. Dallis, 2025
Antibody, Elane Kim, 2026
House of Myth and Necessity, Jennifer A Sutherland, 2026
Scythe, Elizabeth Sylvia, 2026
Fifty Mothers, Preeti Vangani, 2026
The Visible Field, Zoë Ryder White, 2026
Snails of the Apocalypse, Martha Zweig, 2026
Turn a Girl to Salt, Janet McAdams, 2027
Little Automata of the Deciduous Forest, Mirande Bissell, 2027
Whale Garden, Carolyn Oliver, 2027

Plainwater Nonfiction Series

There Is News Along the Ohio River, Beth Gilstrap, 2026
Backyard Alchemy, J.D. Ho, 2026